HAVE YOU SEEN A BLACK BEAR?

Written by
Katie Cate

Illustrated by
Kate Fallahee

For Granddad

Have you seen a black bear?

Make sure to look high and low,

but don't forget to bike real slow.

They climb trees high in the air.

Oh, have you seen a black bear?

Shhh, let's be quiet and listen!

Black bears come when fireflies glisten.

Look near the water. Quick! Over there!

Oh, have you seen a black bear?

At the highest peak when the moon is new,

Where do bears hide?
Next time we'll know.

But for now it's
time for me to go.

Maybe next time
I'll look everywhere.

Maybe next time
I'll see a black bear.

SEARCH AND FIND

Chipmunk

Firefly

Coyote

Barred Owl

Flame Azaleas

Mountain Laurel

Brook Trout

Pileated
Woodpecker

Thyme-Leaved
Bluets

White Tail Deer

Northern
Cardinal

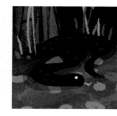

Black Rat Snake

River Otter

Elk

Black-bellied
Salamander

Pipevine
Swallowtail

Eastern
Box Turtle

Catawba
Rhododendron

Canada Warbler